HEARING THE VOICE OF THE CONSUMER

HEARING THE VOICE OF THE CONSUMER

IAN WHITE, MIKE DEVENNEY,
REBA BHADURI, JACK BARNES,
PETER BERESFORD, ADRIANNE JONES

Edited by ISOBEL ALLEN

Policy Studies Institute

PSI Publications are obtainable from all good bookshops, or by visiting the Institute at: 100 Park Village East, London NW1 3SR (01 387 2171).

Sales Representation: Pinter Publishers Ltd.

Individual and Bookshop orders to: Marston Book Services Ltd, P.O. Box 87, Oxford, OX1 1LB.

A CIP catalogue record of this book is available from the British Library.

PSI Discussion Paper 21

ISBN 0 85374 412 2

Printed by Bourne Offset Ltd, Iver, Bucks.

CONTENTS

Preface

This Discussion Paper brings together six papers delivered at the annual ADSS/PSI Seminar held on 26 June 1987 at Policy Studies Institute. The theme was Hearing the Voice of the Consumer.

The aim of the ADSS/PSI seminars is to stimulate debate among practitioners, researchers and policy-makers on the most topical issues in social policy. In recent years, the seminars have looked at the major challenges facing social services departments of increasing collaboration between health and social services and the developing relationship between the private and public sectors in the provision of social care.

But the voice of the consumer has become louder and more demanding and the 1987 seminar examined the implications for social services departments not only of hearing the voice of the consumer but also of acting upon what is heard.

What is the consumer saying? And who is the consumer in any case? The demands for more participation in the planning and provision of social services are coming from users of services, from carers and from local communities more generally. Their views may not always coincide.

How far, and how fast, and in what ways can social services departments respond? What kind of partnership can social services departments build up with the local community and with the people within it? And what are the implications of increasing 'consumerism' for the future? These were some of the questions posed in the seminar. The papers from the seminar are being published by Policy Studies Institute to bring the discussion to a wider audience.

The seminar was funded by the Joseph Rowntree Memorial Trust and the ADSS/PSI Group greatly value the continuing support of the Trust.

Isobel Allen

Policy Studies Institute

1. Consumer Influences: Challenges for the Future

Ian White

Director of Social Services, London Borough of Hillingdon

> *Probably the most important management fundamental that is being ignored today is staying close to the customer to satisfy his needs and anticipate his wants. In too many companies, the customer has become a bloody nuisance whose unpredictable behaviour damages carefully made strategic plans, whose activities mess up computer operations, and who stubbornly insists that purchased products should work (Lew Young, Editor-in-Chief, Business Week).*

Introduction

Talk of consumer influence, getting closer to the customer and such phrases are among the latest vogues in social services. The above quotation, taken from *In Search of Excellence*[1], nevertheless carries many messages for service organisations like social services and poses questions about how effective we are in hearing our consumers. The advent of 'excellence', together with the emergence of and renewed interest in decentralisation by the larger political parties, a thrust of government thinking encapsulated in various Acts and Circulars aimed at 'giving back power to the people', together with considerable amounts of written material, all seem to indicate that the idea of consumer influences on the large welfare bureaucracies has gained a foothold that it has never had before. Recent government initiatives, such as the proposals for the management of schools by governors, the *rights* to a written assessment contained in the Disabled Persons Act and the proposals for the reform of child care law, in relation to the rights of parents and local authorities, all give very clear messages about a style of thinking aimed at giving a different balance of power between consumers and the welfare bureaucracies.

Why has this subject got on the agenda now and why is it felt necessary for central direction influencing what ought to be the very basis of good operating practice in service organisations? Furthermore, this subject is receiving a level of debate as if it had never been debated before. It is almost as though this is a brand new idea that we must start learning about when, in fact, ideas and good practice involving consumer influence have been with us from the very beginning.

Looking around the country, there are innumerable examples already effective in many different forms. Quite clearly, however, there is not a *consistency* of thinking and action across the country and I certainly hope that this seminar and the Discussion Paper will help focus on the issues we need to think about to ensure the development of effective consumer influence within our services.

This is, essentially, a personal view - the view of a working director of social services who has had to stop and think about his own operations. I hope this paper touches on the main points that are of concern to us all. It does not pretend to be all-encompassing.

Definitions

Social services departments are involved with the most dependent people in our communities. Very broadly, these people are the least able to communicate well, understand complex bureaucracies and have the confidence to take on the so-called 'professionals'. They are children, old people, disabled people, people with different ethnic backgrounds, all of whom rely on us to help with many of their everyday-life problems. This dependency is not an equal partnership - how could it be, given that one person is dependent on the other? On one level, therefore, consumer influence is about addressing the question of *equality* in a way which helps people challenge judgements, views and plans. It is about helping people keep control over decision-making about their lives.

Our 'clients', however, are not the only people within my definition of 'consumer'. I tend to think about consumers on a much broader base and I include in this parents and relatives who are often the carers; small groups of people who come together as self-help groups; established local and national voluntary organisations; foster parents and adopters and those people who, in other jargon terms, might be 'service givers'. For the purpose of this paper, therefore, I am thinking broadly rather than narrowly since, in my view, each of these consumers will share some common ground but also different aspirations for influencing our large welfare bureaucracies.

Services and the future
A further starting point is to consider society today and in the foreseeable future, because the consumers of today might not, necessarily, be the same as the consumers of tomorrow. As a director, I have to ask myself whether today's services, many of which were developed ten to fifteen years ago, are responsive to today's society and today's needs. For example, how can a home help service, developed ten years ago and delivering an average of two and a half hours per week of practical care, be relevant to a society where the proportion of elderly people over 75 is going to increase by 43 per cent and whose needs are, primarily, for care outside the usual employment hours of 9 am to 1 pm? How is it that we can live with our inherited services and not understand the changing needs around us? Why have the consumers of that service not influenced us earlier? I wonder how many directors and senior managers, as well as politicians, meet consumers face to face regularly to ask them whether the services that we are delivering are relevant to their needs, whether we are accessible, friendly and able to be influenced?

A recent BBC TV *Brass Tacks* programme highlighted three important issues for carers and clients alike:

- the poor information available about what help there is;

- the 'disjunction' between their needs and the help there was available;

- the lack of influence they felt they had over social services departments and the 'unfriendly' contacts they had with departments.

For these people, our services were crude, inaccessible, frightening, leaving them with a feeling of helplessness.

Society is changing rapidly and social services departments are going to face many new challenges in future. Major strategies such as 'care in the community' are changing the way we think about traditional services and the role of clients in society. Changes in the age structure of the population mean that we cannot work with outdated services and that we need to test out with our consumers our assumptions about their needs rather than developing alternative strategies without reference to them. How many reports go to social services committees about service development which do not mention the outcome of consultation with clients, voluntary groups and consumers in the widest sense? We need to build a discipline into our work which engages us in better forms of consultation.

The birthrate is falling: two-thirds of women over 35 work; one-third of marriages end in divorce; 17 per cent of births are outside marriage. These statistics from a recent article in *The Economist* challenge the concept that the traditional family can be the basic building block of our society. *The Economist* estimated that, perhaps, only 10 per cent of families fell into this definition.

For social services, the implications are serious. If the traditional family unit is disappearing, complete with its support, its help and advice, then there will be many parents with little support who need a great deal of help. Social services are, for example, going to have to re-think the basis of their policies for under-fives and the thrust of basic child care work which is often relative and rooted in statutory work. The vacuum created by changes in family structure need filling by help tailored to people's needs when they need it. Instead of waiting for crises to occur, we will need an approach which provides real help to prevent such crises. In other words: early support partnerships. Our image is making us *more* remote and threatening. In response, many of us are now setting up parent support groups so as to build an infrastructure of support in place of traditional family units. We are providing good quality parenting advice to the community to help people over difficult patches by, for example, running 'night school classes' for people struggling with the problems of adolescent children. In effect, we are analysing our work and building better preventive systems as a response to the changes in society and the needs these changes throw up.

Similarly, how well are we hearing the voice of children in these critical cases? How many of us are really credible to this group in our community? How is it that we have become so remote and so feared, that children, in desperation, do not feel able to telephone or contact the social services but need instead to go to other agencies or keep their fears to themselves? We are certainly not close to them and we need to think hard about how to change this image and develop a welcoming and acceptable face to our services.

In mental handicap, different challenges are emerging. The 'Care in the Community' strategy is encouraging us to make plans for people who have lived for many years in long-stay, single-sex, isolated wards, now to be looked after in the community, often in multi-sex, small units. This change in policy raises for us many challenges about how such units are run and our attitudes towards the people who live in them. We will need explicit policies about sensitive personal matters such as giving sex education to mentally handicapped people. We will need to go public on the problems of risks that are associated with independent living and greater client self-determination. The Sunderland case raises serious questions about the consumer's voice versus society's fears. Our authority has now embarked on a public education campaign to address some of these issues. We will stop being just providers and become partners in care. We will re-think our ways of working and will need to have regular meetings with parents' groups, voluntary organisations and disabled people themselves.

Today, many severely disabled babies are born who, only a few years ago, would have died at birth. They have life expectancies and caring needs significantly different from the clients that we have been traditionally used to caring for. How are we going to hear their views about their preferences for the way they live, what they do, how they are treated? Are we going to be competent to care for them properly? How are we going to hear the voice of their parents and deliver help tailored to their particular needs? Ideas such as parents being trainers are now being developed. I applaud such developments and see them as beacons for the future and the basis for a public acceptance that we do not always know best and that care in the future is going to be real partnership.

The increase in the number of disabled people living in the community in small units poses other questions. How will we know if they are happy or not? How will we know when they are being maltreated, given that they live in small units with people who appear, to them, to be very powerful and influential? This raises a challenge for care management and poses the question about how we ensure that safety valves exist for people in these situations to express worries and concerns. The growth of the advocacy movement is clearly critical, but I believe it needs to go a lot further than it has done until now. Advocates could be external to our departments. Parents and friends could play a key role in the operation of these ideas.

Elderly people in the future will live longer and become more frail. Yet, only five per cent of the over-75s live in institutions; 70 per cent live alone or with their partners; 25 per cent with relatives and friends. How well do we hear the views of elderly people in old people's homes who have to share rooms with three or more others, after living a life in traditional family units? Do we ever ask them what their views are? Do we really encourage them to have choices? How do we hear their fears and their preferences? How many homes have spent time setting up mechanisms for residents' meetings, advocacy, for improvements in menu planning and the management of the home? How many homes are still run round staff rotas, traditional working practices, inflexible job descriptions and so on, rather than starting from what residents want?

How many of us consult clients who get the home help service to see whether the times that we are programming the home help to visit are convenient? I wonder how many of us systematically review what home helps are doing and ask clients whether the service they are getting is what they believe they need?

Significantly, however, and despite the sums of money involved, social services only get to a small proportion of the elderly population. The majority of elderly people live alone or with partners or relatives and friends, and, as they get older and frailer, will need major and increasing care. How many of us have explicit policies for supporting carers so as to make their lives more manageable? How many of us even have the slightest idea of the burdens of caring for heavily dependent elderly people in our local areas and have gone to the trouble of trying to find out? How many of us encourage the carers to have a more relaxed relationship with us, where we can respond to their crises and their needs as well as the person they are caring for? How many of us meet carers, or do we leave them alone to get on with their lives?

I also wonder about society's attitudes when it comes to consumer influence. How many elderly people, living alone and probably with deteriorating mental faculties, are forced - by so-called caring relatives or professionals - into living in old people's homes against their will so as to remove from the community embarrassment and risk? In my experience, society, friends, professionals, seem to think that the consumer would be better with their lives taken over for them, rather than living their own style of life into old age. How do we hear the voice of that old person and how do we reconcile it with the voices of others who wish to remove problems from sight? What public education programmes are we engaging in to create a climate of understanding and to remove some of the myths of old age?

People with disabilities are today living longer lives than ever before. They are a challenge to us in helping them lead normal lives, and yet I wonder how many of us effectively hear their voice. We have our traditional services, but how many of us are negotiating substantially new housing so they can live normal lives? The advance of 'high-tech' technology opens up endless possibilities for disabled people to help them compensate for the effects of their disability. How many of us are reviewing the potential for adapting new technology as part of our services? What are we doing to innovate in this field and to bring new technology to their door in order to assist them?

Parents and friends carry a tremendous burden looking after disabled children and adults for many years. They give a lifetime to the care of their family and are more knowledgeable than we are about their needs, and yet we leave them to do it with very few policies for supporting carers and for working on their behalf to reduce the stresses of their family lives. We should be setting up advice centres, carers' groups, support schemes, all aimed at supporting them.

The voice of minority groups is starting to be heard, yet how many of us hear that voice effectively when their political lobby is so dispersed and our traditional services are unlikely to be relevant? How competently are we reviewing our services in the light of these new consumer needs? How many of us systematically encourage minority groups to help us re-think the social services for them? How many of us involve such groups in the implementation of our services?

Our future consumers are going to be all of these people, and more. They are going to be people suffering from Aids, for whom we have very little knowledge about the type of service that is best provided, and about whom society has very confused views; they are going to be people suffering from varieties of mental illness for whom community care is often extremely insensitive. The challenge to us is to ask ourselves whether what we are doing at the moment is relevant to them, and, if not, how can we change it?

Organisational issues

Consumer influence is also a challenge to the way we organise ourselves and to the way professions have traditionally set themselves up. State welfare is a large and complex process, hard to understand, mainly used by those least able to understand it. It is a field of jargon, law, and is staffed at times by people with low morale and rather poor credibility. At times we all feel we are managing a service which is on the defensive and one which is not putting out a confident face encouraging those people in most need to involve themselves with us. Society in the future is going to be one which demands increasing control by individuals over their own lives and on decisions made about them.

People are, rightly, going to be less afraid to challenge professionals and are going to be more vocal in their preferences. This trend raises a number of questions for us:

(a) How accessible are our services - do people know how to get to us - is it easy? Is our publicity good and do we offer a pleasant public face to the public? If we do not, people will not feel encouraged to deal with us and we will end up remote, defensive and increasingly 'dinosaur-like'.

(b) Can our clients influence the type of service they get? To what extent do we consult with clients about the type of service they get and their needs, or do we effectively offer a service which is only 'we know best'? To what extent do we consult with individual clients with our case planning? Do we have systematic reviews of their needs, involvement in case conferences, or do we carry out all these professional/technological processes in the absence of the recipients of the service?

(c) Are we organised in such a way that services can be shaped to the individual aspirations and the peculiarities of local areas? Do social services staff link with the local community? Do they know all the local networks and the key people in those communities and, by dint of that, become equally accepted as part of that local community, or are we still a 'faceless' bureaucracy? If we believe that we are part of the local community, how effectively can local people and local groups influence us? What mechanisms are there for discussions, consultations and external challenge to the effectiveness of our services?

(d) How can we ensure that consumers, and consumer groups, influence service planning for the future? We have to question how well our policy making processes hear the consumer at that stage. How often is our response either bureaucratic, or token?

I make no apologies for quoting from *In Search of Excellence*:

The excellent companies are the better listeners. They get a benefit from client closeness and most of their real innovation comes from their clients ... Successful firms pay more attention to their customer than do failures. Successful innovators innovate in response to customer needs, involve potential users in the development of the innovation and understand user needs better.

I believe that this encompasses the sort of process that we ought to be engaging in and I do not think we do it well.

(e) How confident do clients feel in accessing our system? How many of us have implemented client access to files policies and how is it that despite initiatives on this front, it has still taken Archy Kirkwood MP to promote a Bill to fully implement this idea?

Similarly, how many of us have got effective complaints procedures as proposed by the National Consumer Council (NCC) which have been discussed publicly and are well publicised and used effectively? Successful organisations do not just have complaints procedures as a bureaucratic necessity but encourage consumers to 'complain' or 'comment' in the widest possible sense about their services. The outcome of this information should be analysed by management. How many of us report to our committees systematically on complaints and how many of us encourage people to tell us how we can best improve our services? Not many I think.

The implications for us are significant since they imply a very different style from that most traditionally found in local government. It implies a confident relationship style and one which is unafraid of being criticised and challenged. It implies an organisation which is confident about its ability to communicate what it is trying to do and the paradoxes it is often faced with. It implies an approach which goes to the very heart of training of our staff since it implies that we will need to teach people how to innovate, how to communicate in a different way, and how to be unafraid of client influence.

Social services departments, at the end of the day, are part of the political processes. They are accountable to political control and elected councillors, each of whom have their own different philosophies and ideologies. Many councillors feel that it is their job to represent the voice of the consumer but, clearly, this would be an impossibility, given the range of activity of local government and of social services in particular. The challenge for the future also, therefore, is a challenge for councillors to find ways which, on the one hand uphold their role but, on the other hand, allow their policies and practices to be argued about by consumers as well as by particular lobbies. It is well known that the social services lobby is very weak by the very nature of its clientele.

Conclusion

I would conclude by suggesting that social services should review their operations to ensure the following eight objectives are met:

(1) that we have a welcoming 'face' and a form of organisation which is clearly accessible and understandable: a service with well-trained staff, good publicity and information; a service which people want to come to, not escape from;

(2) that we provide good quality information about what help can be given - and, equally important, fair explanations when services cannot be provided;

(3) that we provide services which fit consumers' needs when they are needed and which are flexible, not services and working practices stuck in history and geared to reactive work alone;

(4) that every opportunity is given to clients to control decisions over their lives and to complain effectively if they are not satisfied; in effect, a service which is open and honest, not closed and defensive;

(5) that we give consumers a real influence in changing policies and services through real involvement; it implies councillors, staff and clients working together in partnership;

(6) that we lead thinking about the potential for our consumers to benefit from the possibilities of advances in medical and electronic technology; that we provide a service which does the 'pathfinding' for the least able in our society;

(7) that we provide a voice in society to help the community understand consumers' problems;

(8)   that we work actively to help develop a society which doesn't lock handicapped and elderly people out of sight, but which is tolerant and caring.

The implications of these ideas are far-reaching. They will affect our everyday lives. Confident political and professional leadership in social services departments across the country is going to be critical.

Reference
1.   T.J. Peters and R.H. Waterman, *In Search of Excellence: lessons from America's best-run companies,* Harper and Row, 1983.

2. Consumer-led Services: Fashionable Dogma or Practical Necessity?

Mike Devenney

Vice-Chair of Social Services, London Borough of Islington

The failure of social services departments to develop a coherent and consistent method of service delivery is manifest. The misery and waste which results in people's lives beggars description. The idea that consumer-led social services would help provide a more effective and responsive service delivery model is by no means new. This notion emerged in the late 1960s and has hung around social service departments ever since - some may say like a rope around a condemned prisoner.

As a politician I will not attempt to catalogue, compare or assess the various models of consumer-led services that have been tried with varying degrees of success. The social service professionals and academics can do that quite adequately. What I intend to do in this short paper is to try to give some political context to the problems of consumer-led services and suggest how it may be possible to move forward on the matter.

It may be wise at this point to take a moment or two to consider how we define consumer-led services and what are the main parameters of the issue. The 'clients' or 'users' of personal social services departments are our consumer group. The 'user' group spans a huge spectrum ranging from families, children, elderly people, to people with disabilities. In fact, it would be fair to say that the user group is potentially all the communities in any service area. The 'professionals' involved are essentially all the staff resources of the department with particular emphasis on field workers. One must remember that these staff are potentially users as well, so that the distinction between the professional and the client is somewhat arbitrary and rests upon the rather dubious notion of professionalism based on training, codes of practice and ethics.

In political terms the distinction may be said to rest more upon class and economic power. The services in question include the whole gamut of social services provision, from residential care to field social work to care for under-fives. It should be noted at this point that, in most instances, social services do not operate in a vacuum, and that inter-departmental factors are very important and have an enormous impact on the final shape of the service delivered. However, this is an issue in itself and warrants an in-depth examination which we do not have time to do justice to here.

Finally, a definition, or at least setting the parameters, of consumer-led services may help set the scene and help to avoid confusion. In the context of this discussion, consumer-led will be taken to mean the ability of the user group of the service to influence, change, direct or control the policy development of service delivery practices in order to reflect and meet their changing needs more effectively. One may think that this is a rather open-ended definition. This is deliberately so, as consumer-led services must operate on a range of levels and should not be restricted to a narrow interpretation or a single mode of practice.

Political origins of consumerism in social services, in my opinion, have run parallel with the development of welfare provision. With the advent of the Attlee/Butler welfare ethos there arose a paternalistic bureaucracy which did not attempt to take on board the possibility of the client having a voice. The system knew best, and if the 'punters' received what they needed, why confuse matters? In the immediate post-war era this model became well established and served its purpose. The consumer goods boom had just begun to flourish and the new 'consumers' were just beginning to recognise their needs and their ability to have them met.

Throughout the 1950s and early 1960s, welfare and health services became increasingly sophisticated, as did the consumer. These developments were founded on the economic boom during this period and an insatiable demand by the public for new goods and services. The mid-1960s brought about the rise of the civil rights movement. First, the black movement in the United States of America struggled against race discrimination. The impetus of this movement spilled over into a new social consciousness leading to the revival of the women's movement and the birth of the disability movement. Running counter to these civil rights campaigns was the increasing professionalisation of welfare and health services, thus alienating many people from the services they needed and wanted. However, in the late 1960s and early 1970s the people and ideas of the civil rights era began to permeate the system causing a feeling of restlessness to creep through the previously self-assured caring professions. The unchallenged 'right' of the professional to decide what a client needed was gently being called into question and the role of the client became a major debating point. In the early 1970s, with the outcome of the Seebohm Report and the consequent restructuring of health and welfare services, the newly-formed departments of social services took on an innovative image with increased public accountability. Much of the 1970s were spent coming to terms with new local authority structures and developing more effective models of service delivery.

The late 1970s saw the emergence of equal opportunities policies in Labour-controlled authorities. This was in many ways the rise of 'metropolitan socialism', which was personified by the Greater London Council. The application of equal opportunities principles was gradually extended to all local authority services. With the publication of the Barclay Report in 1982, the role of clients and their rights was firmly put on the political agenda. It is interesting to note that the Barclay Report spoke about neighbourhood social services several years before any social services department decentralised its services. In my view, the link between the development and the implementation of equal opportunities and issues of consumer-led services is fundamentally important.

'Equal opportunities' is not merely a string of moral imperatives. It is a functional prerequisite of planning and developing an economic and effective service network. Without this pragmatic and targeted approach to service planning, an authority - in particular a social services department - will embark, willy-nilly, on a course which will progressively disconnect the Council from the real needs of the community, thus exposing the most vulnerable in our community. An integral component of this equal opportunity strategy must be the involvement of the communities in the decision-making process.

Some may say that equal opportunities and, therefore, consumer-led services have become a fashionable dogma espoused by 'self-styled' radical local authorities, many of whom are Labour-controlled inner city authorities with complex social and economic dilemmas. At first glance one may think that giving credence to consumer-led services in this hostile political and social environment would further compound the problems of dwindling resources, increasing demand, high levels of poverty and negligible government support.

Would it not be more straightforward and efficient to allow the politicians and the professionals to decide what priorities are to be set and how resources are best allocated? The general ethos of the professional in our society already contains a number of unavoidable difficulties. The professional policeman is not constrained by the diktats of the criminal, and the student does not determine the curriculum. Why then support the thesis that social services delivery should be qualitatively and quantitatively determined by the user of the service? If the domain of the professional in social services is to be trespassed by the user, then are we undermining the trained and experienced human resource made available to the department? Are we replacing the objective judgement of the professional with the *ad hoc* subjective amateur judgement of the client? In my view, the care and welfare of the community is too important a matter to be left in the hands of the politician or the professional.

I would suggest that there is a distinct and vital tripartite division of roles: the rights of the client, the responsibilities of the manager, and the accountability of the politician. If this formula for combining these three roles is ill-conceived there will be disruption in the community. The manager and the politician will have failed, but the client alone will pay the price for that failure. Without the mechanics to provide the community feedback, professional practices and evaluation will be further forced into dogma and jargon - while outside in the real world the current consensus against the performance and value of social services will take further hold and increasingly resemble the worst knocking copy of the gutter press. Each lurid distorted story of human tragedy is laid at the doors of the social services departments who have not, apparently, interfered enough when, for the rest of the time, they have interfered too much.

The hidden assumption prevalent among many professions is that demand is generated by need, and that need is only experienced by those helpless sections of the community which cannot help themselves and who are therefore unable to take part in any formulation of policy or targeting of provision. This nonsensical variant of social Darwinism relates to a homogeneous mass of people who are not fit enough to survive without the passive consumption of support expertly supplied by the professional according to the priorities of the politician.

Of course the reality is that there are many kinds of need reflecting an infinite range of historical disadvantage. How can the professionals then assess and exercise their skills without detailed local understanding? This is vital in order to identify the true needs of the community and not those preconceived by training or dogma. And again, without this local community input, how can the politician evaluate priorities? Without the active participation of the users at the point of need, the professional may scatter valuable resources into a void and the politician operate in a vacuum. Without decentralisation of control and information based on mutual cooperation, can the user and professional fully achieve their common goal of having needs met?

In Islington we have undertaken a total programme of decentralisation of services. In practical terms this means we have 24 local neighbourhood offices which offer most of the major Council services. The major components of these offices are social services and housing. From the clients' point of view the neighbourhood office offers a one-stop shop. The Council is now in the process of developing active neighbourhood forums made up of elected members of the community and local organisations who will, in the long term, have an increasing say in how services are delivered in that area and contribute to the overall policy-making process. Superimposed on this decentralised structure is a user-group based system of sub-committees concerning people with physical and learning disabilities, people with mental problems, the elderly, and children and families. These sub-committees are made up of users of their respective services and are given some officer support. These sub-committees directly input into the main committees of the Council. In addition, there are co-opted members of most disadvantaged groups on all Council committees. Together these three layers of participation provide the Council with valuable information and expertise, and at the same time afford the user some degree of autonomy.

This model of decentralisation promotes a number of important principles. First, it allows the user to have some choice in service provision. Secondly, it allows a planned process of consultation to take place so that the differing needs of the community can be equally met. Thirdly, it allows the easy transmission of information between the Council and the user about what services are available. Also it allows the user to inform the Council of specific needs. Fourthly, it allows the basic concept of participation to take place by all on an equal basis. Finally, it allows the users to have some autonomy over how they use the service.

From the service provider's point of view the major benefit must be seen in terms of a more responsive and accountable service. I would go so far as to argue that decentralisation offers the only sound managerial and financial strategy for service delivery in the current economic and political climate. If the services are in the community and accountable to the consumer they will have more chance of being protected and improved. In my view, it must be a practical necessity for local authorities to engage the active participation of the community.

This partnership has a dual role. In the short-term it will help mitigate what I see as the worst implications of the government's financial strategy and will help to maintain strong local accountability by which the local authority is able to build upon, and to maintain service. In the long-term it will provide the basis for an integrated system of consumer-led services.

References

1. Nicholas Murray, 'Giving the client a voice', in *Community Care*, 16 September 1982.

2. Wendy Ball, 'Local authority policy-making on equal opportunities: corporate provision, co-option and consultation', in *Policy and Politics*, Vol.15, No.2, 1987.

3. The Prince of Wales Advisory Group on Disability, *Living options guideline for those planning services for people with severe physical disabilities*, 1985.

4. Simon Brisenden, 'Independent living and the medical model of disability', in *Disability, Handicap and Society*, Vol.1, No.2, 1986.

5. Joseph Katan and Edward Prager, 'Consumer and worker participation in agency-level decision-making; some considerations of their linkages', in *Administration in Social Work*, Vol.10(1), Spring 1986.

3. Race and Culture: the 'Invisible' Consumers

Reba Bhaduri

Principal Teacher/Supervisor, Medical Social Work Department, Withington Hospital, City of Manchester

The aim of this paper is to highlight the low uptake of social services by the Afro-Caribbeans and people from the Indian sub-continent. It will address issues such as: Are the black minority community not aware of the services provided by social services departments? Is this a reflection of a general lack of public awareness of what social services have to offer? Are social services departments aware of and willing to reach out for the minority communities? Does the answer lie in a closer partnership between minority voluntary organisations and social services? What are the implications for staff training in race and culture?

The paper raises more questions than it can hope to answer. Professor J.E. Mayer and N. Timms wrote in 1970: 'The social services ... are rapidly expanding to meet an increasing number of social needs. Yet we are profoundly ignorant about the ways in which the consumers of these services respond to social work help that the community makes available'[1]. The Short Report (1984/85) outlined the central aim of community care in the future as 'matching the services with consumers rather than vice-versa'[2].

Despite the growing concern that the opinion of clients or consumers about what they think we do or fail to do must be of great significance there is relatively little data on consumers' views.

Developing a consumer orientation requires that the population knows something about the services that may be available. Do they? For example, in 1974-6 I did research on mental health clients' perception of mental health services from the old mental health department and then from the social services department following the Seebohm reorganisation. The majority of clients showed confusion in their knowledge and understanding of social services and of the services available to them [3] [4].

Going beyond this, there is hardly any research involving people who do not come to the attention of services: the 'invisible' consumers. I will look specifically at those who come from a different race and culture. All kinds of assumptions are used by policy makers, administrators and practitioners about the ways in which consumers approach certain services, see their problems and so on. But these assumptions have rarely been critically examined.

For example, let us look at Asian elderly and Afro-Caribbean elderly people.

Assumptions

(1) They are most likely to go 'home' (to their country of origin) after retirement.

(2) Asian families will always care for their ageing dependants.

(3) Their numbers are not significant enough to warrant attention.

What is the actual outcome of these assumptions? There is hardly any service delivery or there is inappropriate service delivery to these groups.

For the majority of Afro-Caribbean and Asian elderly people, Britain is a second home or a third home rather than the country of their birth.

Their expectations of old age were shaped in Africa, the West Indies and the Indian sub-continent, where both the lifestyle and the status of the elderly are very different from those in Britain. Whatever the indigenous elderly may suffer in this society (that is poverty, isolation, loneliness, bad housing), the Afro-Caribbean and the Asian elderly suffer more. They have to live with racial and cultural prejudice.

For my second example, infant mortality is high amongst Asians. Dr Lumb's comparative study of Asian and UK European maternity patients in Bradford (1974/78) showed that the perinatal mortality rate for Asian babies was persistently higher than for babies born to UK European mothers [5].

I have not come across any social work literature which deals with the challenge of offering grief counselling to people from a different culture [6]. On the contrary, I hear comments from workers such as 'the families are so supportive that they do not need social work help' or 'we don't want to intrude on their religious and cultural practice following bereavement'. The result is that there is no service delivery to these groups.

I am compelled to raise basic questions about the underlying body of knowledge in social work. We need to re-examine the over-emphasis on pathology, especially psycho-pathology, in our teaching and social work theories. In the process of assessing clients, I feel that more attention is paid to weaknesses and limitations than to strength of personality and inner resources. We need to shift the focus in social work education from pathology to human strength, resources and potentialities. Richard Pinder commented, 'The achievement of more satisfactory outcomes to social work with ethnic minority clients depends not so much on isolating the cultural differences of clients or on combating the racism of workers, as on instilling in workers the confidence to avoid turning the positive capacity to *differ* that ethnic minority clients necessarily display into a *negative* quality of resistance' [7]. In other words we need not view ethnic or racial differences in a problematic way.

I am not surprised that Afro-Caribbean or Asian people are so reluctant to ask for services they are entitled to, even if they are aware of the services. As a result they may come to the notice of helping agencies too late. For example, clients from the Indian sub-continent who are suffering from depression are likely to go to their GPs or to no one [8]. Why are the Afro-Caribbean clients more likely to be admitted under compulsory admission rather than voluntary admission? Why do young Afro-Caribbeans appear more frequently in court than in clinics? Why are there more black Afro-Caribbean mentally-ill clients ending up in secure units?

Social work with black or Asian clients demands not another specialism to meet the special needs, but a radical re-working of the standard and conventional framework of service delivery.

Consumers could become involved in the planning and management of their services and managers need to become more democratic. For example, they need to liaise closely with various minority organisations to identify service gaps.

Black clients like all other clients have the same need for an appropriate and sensitive service. However, black people may have to travel a longer and harder route to achieve this.

We need to remember that the client may feel relatively powerless and that the worker and the client may not share the same lifestyle perspective due to class, culture, and racial differences. Despite original social work emphasis on openness, there is more evidence of defensiveness, game playing, innuendo and avoidance of issues in the course of client/worker interaction. Social workers have a responsibility to encourage explicitness and to clarify mutual expectations about the services and functions of the agencies. In my experience, I find social workers are reluctant to talk about racial issues with clients. Yet this may be the uppermost thought in the clients' minds. Moreover social workers tend to feel uncomfortable about asking questions they will normally ask a UK/European client in case they appear racist. What is the outcome? It can lead to wrong assessment, not an honest relationship and an ineffective service delivery.

We need to grasp more sympathetically the difficulties that face practitioners. For example, what do we do when working with an Asian teenage girl asking to be received into care in the face of apparent family pressure to consider marriage? Does the worker execute traditional child care policy or enter the dangerous world of cultural intrusion? Social workers do not have in-depth training on racial and cultural aspects of social work either in the basic qualifying course or in the department at post-qualifying level. I have reservations about racial awareness training or anti-racist training without its being accompanied by the examination of practice and policy issues.

We must not forget that clients' views will help to maintain accountability, identify service gaps, influence policy formulation and decision making and also initiate changes within a specific agency or within the broader service delivery system.

By focussing on what clients think and comparing their views with those of practitioners we can identify crucial issues and their significance for policy making, for practice delivery, for education and for training and research.

I would like to finish my paper with some positive news. Several community organisations have pioneered support services for Afro-Caribbean and Asian people. However these support services are far from being comprehensive owing to lack of funding and liaison with statutory services. In order to offer an appropriate service delivery, social services need to work in closer partnership with community organisers. I was pleased to find that the Social Services Inspectorate has accorded priority to the subject of race and culture. They have undertaken studies in the Midlands, West Yorkshire, London and the North-West region. I would like to recommend the North-West study, the 1986 report, *Social Services for Ethnic Minorities - Policy and Practice in the North-West.* This is a study of interviews with senior managers in 17 social services departments. The study focussed on policy issues [9]. I was delighted to take part in the second phase of the study in the North-West on practice delivery. The report is not ready yet. It will make stimulating reading.

We must not be apathetic and forget that a significant group of people are suffering. The policy makers, the trainers and the practitioners all need to get their acts together. Trainers and managers need to give practitioners the confidence to follow through with their practice skill when working with different racial and cultural groups. The practitioners have a responsibility to feed back to the managers, policy makers and trainers what they are learning from the clients. The policy makers need to seek out the minority organisations to identify service gaps and to help plan appropriate services in the future. Professional associations and educational bodies need to undertake research on consumers' views. After all, we all have one thing in common: we do care.

References
1. J.E. Mayer & N.Timms, *The Client Speaks*, Routledge and Kegan Paul, 1970, p.2.

2. House of Commons Social Services Committee (Chairman Renee Short) Session 1984-85, Second report, *Community care with special reference to adult mentally ill and mentally handicapped people*, HMSO, 1985, 3 vols.

3. R. Bhaduri, *A Study of Mental Health Social Services in Salford for 1950-74*, M.A. Thesis, Manchester University, 1976.

4. R. Bhaduri, 'The Client Speaks in Salford', *Community Care*, 31 May 1979, pp.19-21.

5. K.M. Lumb, and others, 'A comparative review of Asian and British born maternity patients in Bradford 1974-87', *Journal of Epidemiology and Community Health*, June 1981, Vol.35, No.2, pp.106-109.

6. R. Bhaduri, 'Patient minority', *Social Work Today*, 27 February 1984, pp.18-19.

7. R. Pinder, 'Respecting Differences - The Ethnic Challenge to Social Work Practice', *Social Work Today*, 8 February 1983, pp.10-15.

8. M.F. Hussain and J. Gomersall, 'Affective Disorder in Asian Immigrants', *Psychiatria Clinica*, 1978 11(2), pp.87-89.

9. *Social Services for Ethnic Minorities: Policy and Practice in the North-West.* A report of interviews with senior managers in seven-

teen Social Services Departments. R.D. Hughes, Social Services Inspectorate, DHSS, 1986.

4. The Social Services Inspectorate's Work on Using Social Services

Jack Barnes

Deputy Chief Inspector, Social Services Inspectorate, presented the paper based on work by a team of inspectors from the SSI.

We might all agree the importance for the personal social services of sensitivity to the needs and perceptions of the service user. People needing the services are unlikely to be powerful or articulate; and sensitive efforts need to be made to hear what they have to say, and to help them to have their say. Staff providing the services work in an environment which theoretically supports sensitivity to the user. The values of social work, which underpin much of the provision of service, affirm the rights and dignity of the people who use the social services, and the respect they should enjoy.

We might also agree that provision in practice all too often falls short of aspiration. Institutionalised relationships between service-giver and receiver, professional shortsightedness and municipal or charitable paternalism all too often conspire to stigmatise the recipient of services.

The Social Services Inspectorate's contribution to this seminar is to give an early report of some work that has been done to identify ways in which social services agencies across the country are trying to develop and build user-sensitive services. The report is a preliminary account. It does not necessarily represent the views of the Department of Health and Social Security.

During 1987 a small team of Inspectors has been looking in some detail at how five social services departments, and one medium-sized voluntary organisation, were going about improving their sensitivity to the wishes of the users of their service provision. (The Inspectors considered the use of the terms client, consumer, customer in respect of this exercise. User was decided on as a concept for the exercise which did not carry the connotations of other possibilities.) The work has been descriptive and exploratory rather than evaluative. Reports from the fieldwork are available on public access from the DHSS library. An overview report will be prepared.

The exercise was *not* primarily an assessment of the opinions of users, nor of the views of carers, nor of the general public. The Inspectors did not attempt, at this early stage in the work, to consider the issues to do with advocacy for service users. The relationships between elected members and the representatives of users and suppliers of social services were not looked at: nor were the issues of quality of service or of quality assurance.

All of these aspects have their place in a fuller appraisal of the user/consumer dimension to social service provision. But in the initial exercise being described, SSI focussed on the *experience* that people are having of the services today, and have asked:

— how agencies are organising themselves to be more responsive to users;

— what they are trying to do in this respect;

— what difficulties they are experiencing, and how they are attempting to overcome them.

The Inspectorate's findings are best summarised under five headings:

A. provision of *information* to users (potential and actual)

B. *involvement and participation*

C. *choice* issues: choice of what service
choice in *receipt of service*

D. *access* issues: physical access
management process and professional practice

E. *complaints and redress*

Within each of these five aspects we are able:

1. to identify *objectives*: what the agency staff concerned are attempting to achieve;

2. to give *examples* of what is being attempted and achieved in the areas we looked at;

3. to collate *issues which the local staff concerned believe need to be addressed*, and which indeed are being addressed by social services personnel.

A. Information

1. *Objective*:
to inform potential users, in terms acceptable to them,
what personal social services are available,
who is responsible for providing them,
where that person can be found.

2. *Examples found in SSI's work*
Literature

– a range of *leaflets* - distributed within and beyond the agency

– co-ordinated by an information assistant

– *directories* of service available

– covering different needs

– dealing with SSD and health services

- example of payment by commercial sponsorship
- literature in non-English languages
  Local radio and press
- articles and broadcasts featuring the social services
- staff trained to use 'media'
- local radio 'helplines'.

3. *Local assessment of issues to be addressed*

- the need for a budget and staff time for this work;
- is information a spur to excess demands? Can information and early take-up of services help with the prevention of chronic problems?
- what does the varying quality of leaflets tell about agency self image?
- up-dating and restocking of leaflets;
- what is the 'policy' on use of the media - who 'talks for' the agency?
- should information be given on services provided by others i.e. voluntary and private providers?
- is the agency telling users what it wants them to know, or *what they want to know*?

B. Involvement and Participation

1. *Objective*:
   to encourage and expect users to participate in key decisions about the nature of their problem, and what is to be done about it.

2. *Examples found in SSI's work*

   - clear statements of agency expectation about user participation. (We found that these guiding principles provide the context for all else.)

- opening case conferences to, for instance, children, to other users and their carers;

- using a 'contract' approach to provision and receipt of service;

- encouraging the formation of user committees in day and residential services.

3. *Local assessment of issues to be addressed* - the need to clarify roles and expectations:

- who participates in what - participation in child abuse conferences by parents?

- who decides what? What limits are there to what a user group can decide?

- how the agency will respond; how will its response be communicated?

- to whom are agency staff accountable? To what extent can staff act as advocates on behalf of users within the agency.

C. Choice

1. *Objective*:
to ensure potential and actual users have maximum feasible choice about how to have their needs met, and that they retain control over their lives while using social services.

2. *Examples found in SSI's work*

- *when* to use social services (i.e. rotational use of short-term residential care);

- *what type* of service to use (i.e. choice between public or independent residential care; between staying at home or residential care; choice about getting up, going to bed, what to eat within residential care);

- help with *how to use the services* (i.e. lead-in visits to residential care to confirm choice; social work to ensure that the interests of carers and clients are appropriately balanced);

- delaying *irreversible choice* (i.e. keeping options open on return to their own home for people who use residential care).

3. *Local assessment of issues to be addressed*

- preventing staff 'doing things' for service users;

- emphasising to users that they are expected to exercise choice;

- transport;

- geographical/organisational boundaries which are at variance with user preference (patch organisation makes this a particularly sensitive issue).

D. Access

1. *Objective:*
to ensure that users are able to locate, approach and engage with the agency.

2. *Examples found in SSI's work*

- regular checks that sufficient telephone lines are available;

- opening times arranged for the convenience of the users;

- reception rooms arranged similarly;

- location of offices and access points similarly;

- reception and duty staff specifically trained to welcome potential users.

3. *Local assessment of issues to be addressed*

- signposting - good enough to inform, but what of stigmatising effects?

- is intake duty a burden or an opportunity to give service?

- should reception staff be behind the screen?

- can day centres and residential units serve as access points to a range of social services?

E. Complaints

1. *Objective*:
   to formulate, publicise and monitor the use of a clear and manageable procedure for users with cause to be dissatisfied.

2. *Example*
   a leaflet describing *how* to register a complaint, and *what* will happen following the agency's receipt of a complaint.

3. *Local assessment of issues to be addressed*
   Definition: what is a complaint?
   Alternatives: provision of second opinions as alternatives to the use of complaints procedure;
   Publicity:
   more complaints procedures exist than are made known to users;
   Specificity:
   should procedures cover all agency services or be specific to different services?
   Implementation:
   how to keep the process within manageable timescales;
   how to keep complainants informed;
   how to protect complainants;
   how to protect staff;
   how to ensure the case is heard (should friends and advocates be involved);
   What follows:
   types of redress need to be clear;
   appeals and further avenues for complaint.

Making social services user sensitive

We have identified a long list of specific initiatives being taken, and issues being considered, in agencies across the country. Underpinning any successful implementation of these will need to be

− an agreed agency philosophy of user orientation;

− management action to ensure staff understanding and acceptance of the philosophy;

- publicity to make users aware of the attention the agency is paying to respect for their *rights*, and to not eroding their responsibilities.

The 'conventional' ways of directing and developing agency policies are all necessary. These include

- elected member and top management statements of guiding principle;

- service strategies emphasising the rights and responsibilities of users;

- jobs, and job definitions, which focus attention on the need to be sensitive to the user;

- staff training programmes.

But it is also going to be necessary that staff claim the user dimension as their own, and shape agency policy in consequence of it. It is going to be necessary that agencies are prepared to adjust, and to readjust, to the accommodation reached by users and providers of services.

'Making it work' on this occasion does not involve the development of progressively more sophisticated techniques of managing subordinates' behaviour. Rather, the way forward will be found through enhancing the 'self-start' capacity of those service providers who are in direct contact with users.

5. Consumer Views: Data Collection or Democracy?

Peter Beresford

Co-organiser, Battersea Community Action

In this paper I want to look at some of the rationale for hearing the voice of the consumer, some of the ramifications that it has, and practical ways in which agencies and authorities may pursue this objective. To do this I shall draw on findings from four research projects I have been involved in, my own experience as a user of social work services, and my involvement in attempts to enable greater participation for service users and local people in social and other services.

Models for 'hearing the voice of the consumer'
I would like to begin by identifying three approaches or models for hearing the voice of the consumer. For simplicity's sake, let us call these the market research, the consumerist and the democratic approaches.

The first, the market research model, is essentially concerned with information and intelligence gathering. A new sphere of study - client studies - has developed over recent years in response to this need. Underlying it is the idea that if service providers listen to what service users have to say, they are likely to be better equipped to provide efficient and appropriate services.

Second comes the consumerist approach, which I would suggest is an extension of the market research model. Its recent emergence has coincided with the expansion of commercial social services provision. Service users or clients are now conceived of as consumers, and issues are reframed in terms of market preferences, consumer rights and product developments, echoing the language and conceptions of the market economy from which they have been borrowed.

Finally, the democratic approach. This is the model that most interests me. Here the concern is with enabling the involvement of service users so that they may have a greater say in and control over the services that are provided.

I have made clear my own preference among these three models. Other people may have different allegiances. I would, of course, accept that what I have offered represents a crude categorisation - that the reality is more complex and overlapping, but I think this typology can help us make sense of some of the issues involved. The point I am making is that *all* these approaches have their merits. All are legitimate. But they reflect *different* philosophies and intentions. Each of us has to be clear which, if any, we are interested in and to which we wish to commit ourselves and our agency. The problem comes from seeming to offer one when it is another that is intended.

So far in discussions about the voice of the consumer in welfare, we have heard most rhetoric about the third - the democratic approach. Most interest seems to have been expressed in the new consumerism, and, generally, we have not got much beyond information gathering.

Each of these models, of course, has its pros and cons. For example, the market research model is eminently sensible, but it does not carry with it any suggestion of a change in the role or relationship between users and providers in the development of services, and it may disappoint those looking for this or searching for something more than a technical data gathering tool.

The new consumerism may also disappoint some of the expectations surrounding it. These can be predicted from the post-war experience of the consumer movement generally, especially at the lower end of the market, which insofar as they are concerned with people who are poor, social services parallel. Paper rights and public regulations have consistently failed to keep pace with market imperatives in offering people, particularly those with less economic choice, adequate safeguards. The consumerist approach also essentially imposes on rather than responds to users of goods and services. It begins with the *product producer's* needs, not with the consumer's needs. Its concerns are whether people will accept a certain kind of product, whether it should create another need, or present an existing product differently.

Finally, the democratisation of social services might be the most important and right-minded objective, but it is also the most difficult to achieve. So we can expect to encounter all the problems of diversion, dilution and self-deception as we look for large-scale change through rose-tinted glasses. It is this third way, though, that I want to pursue, because if we want to preserve the idea that our society is a social democracy as more than a hopeful myth, then we must work for services that reflect this.

Priority for democratisation in social services
It is not enough for service users to be conceived of as data sources or for our rights as citizens to be reduced to consumer rights. What is at issue is the responsibility of a democratic state to uphold the rights of its citizens. This is as fundamental a matter if we are talking about conditions of life in an old people's home, rights of appeal for parents with children in care or working conditions for people with mental handicaps in adult training centres, as it is for the kinds of issues of human rights that are more often mentioned and for which we weep when we hear of them sacrificed in the Gulag.

There is another equally important, but more specific and highly pragmatic reason for giving priority to democratisation in social services. A key issue in our present public politics is that of individual choice. During the 1980s it appears to have been possible to present collective services as antithetical to individual choice. Taking the example of social services it is not difficult to see why such portrayals have carried conviction. For instance, Suzy Croft and I carried out a research study in East Sussex where there has been the most radical and far-reaching patch decentralisation and move to 'community social work'. Our study was based on a random sample survey of one hundred people in one neighbourhood and fifty group discussions with people from all over Brighton. We found that social services were marginal for most people and that there was a tendency to see them as more suitable for others than for themselves. Most people felt distanced from them and felt that they had little say in them - and that included people using them. People with serious needs and problems would envisage sorting them out for themselves rather than turning to social services [1].

The origins of social services

We need briefly to consider the origins of social services if we are to understand this and move beyond such negative perceptions. Welfare services have never been based on or shaped by a straightforward market supply and demand model - whether or not modified by state intervention. That is because they have rarely represented a straightforward product or service that could be seen as the equivalent of other products or services. The prevailing model instead has been of the state developing services, usually reluctantly because of the resources and intervention they involve, to serve particular functions, primarily for itself and secondly for its citizens. Such functions have been regulatory, custodial, supportive and punitive. They have not been determined by their recipients but by prevailing state fears, philosophies and requirements. So, for example, both the Tudor and Victorian poor laws differentiated between the 'able-bodied' and 'impotent' poor. But the severity with which contemporary accounts show even the latter were treated makes clear such policies were hardly shaped by their interests or demands.

It was in the latter part of the Victorian poor law that choice began to emerge for paupers which was of great importance for the development of social services and this discussion. It was hardly a choice *they* could make. Rather it was one that could be given to them. It rested on the distinction imposed between the 'deserving' and 'undeserving' poor. For those seen as deserving, the option on offer was to receive the services of charitable organisations rather than the poor law. Such organisations, best known of which perhaps was the Charity Organisation Society, have been identified as the founding parents of modern social work. More important they embrace the *paternalist* model of provision at the heart of modern social services and indeed of other welfare state services, like housing, health and education. Here the rigours of the poor law were assuaged by benevolent intentions, but it was still the agenda of their providers which prevailed and there was no suggestion that such services were to enhance the rights or good of their recipients, except in the sense of encouraging their moral or spiritual betterment.

This Victorian choice has a particular resonance in present social services policy. Just as the Victorian pauper might be given the alternative of charitable instead of state provision, so in the 1980s we have heard arguments for a move away from the monopoly of state services towards a plurality of service suppliers including non-statutory, but most emphatically commercial provision.

Of course, as we have seen, for many years there has not been a monopoly of state services. But there is a more fundamental problem in the way of this approach actually enabling greater individual choice. For example, social services departments may make arrangements to provide all three sources of service. But this does not mean that any individual will actually have that choice themselves. For instance, an old person may be offered a place in a commercial old people's home, but they may not be able to opt for a council one because these have increasingly been closed in some areas, or a voluntary one because of their location, greater cost and popularity. Anyway, the person may actually want and need sheltered accommodation or intensive domiciliary support for which resources have not been made available on sufficient scale. And if the individual actually preferred a commercial old people's home, they might not be able to afford it because its charges put it outside the local authority's pocket. A topping-up voucher system may also not help since this old person, like so many others turning to social services, may have little or no money. There is little reason to believe and much evidence to cast doubt on the idea that the dynamics of a mixed economy of welfare will to any extent coincide with or readily be moved to match prevailing patterns of need.

So we are drawn back to the prevailing paternalist model of social services. The Oxford English Dictionary sums up the problem very neatly for us when it comes to individual choice describing such paternalist legislation as that which 'limits the freedom of the subject by well-meant regulations'. More recently feminists have reminded us to treat the word paternalist more carefully at its face value, pointing out that it means a man-made system that is likely to pose particular problems for women - an issue of special importance in social services where most people involved, both as users and workers, are women.

The frequently emphasised shortcomings of paternalist services to enable individual choice have often served to obscure the same failure of the market and market-mix policies. But the problem is still there for collective services. Their paternalism may mean a greater element of philanthropy than is available from other kinds of services. But the lack of effective choice remains.

Individual choice and collective provision

I want to argue for a third way which takes us away from the imposition of social services' paternalist past and the growing inequalities inherent in their increasingly market-led present. The key questions that must be answered are can individual choice be increased and can individual choice and collective provision be reconciled? I would suggest that the answer to both these questions is, yes, and that the prospect for achieving this is offered by increasing the accountability of social services and seeking to democratise them. Making it possible for people to determine what services they have, offers a feasible model for matching services more closely with needs to replace that of supply and demand - which has never really operated in welfare - and of paternalism, which has conspicuously failed. Then services might be truly *demand* based.

However, an important question mark has long been placed over such arguments. People may *not* want such a say. Why burden them with all the difficulties of developing and providing services when all they want is to *use* them? It is an old argument, but one that still gains important support. Most recently I saw it offered by the leader of a London left-Labour local authority [2].

With Suzy Croft and others, I have been involved in several research projects over the last ten years which can help cast some light on the issue. The first project was a study of land-use planning, participation and the meeting of social need, based on a representative sample survey of 580 households in one area [3]. The second was a two-year project with young people including group discussions with them in comprehensive schools, youth clubs, local estates and an unemployment scheme, as well as in-depth interviews with a random sample of fifty school students [4]. The third was a study of children in care in North Battersea drawing on case data for all children in care with a matched interview sample of fifty of the children and young people, their parents, foster parents, social workers and care staff [5]. Finally, the East Sussex study to which I have already referred [6]. All these studies have been concerned with the say and involvement of service users and other local people and there has been a consistency in their findings.

All have encountered a strong sense from most people of having little say in the services affecting them. This lack of control has been experienced as a problem. It has also been associated with widespread complaints and reservations about the appropriateness and quality of services. We do not know from these findings what the relationship is between people's dissatisfaction with services and their feelings of a lack of control over them. We cannot say firmly whether there is a causal connection although some people certainly made the link.

Second, all these studies, except that of children in care where the issue was not raised, offer further evidence to suggest that there is a widespread demand amongst service users and other citizens for greater say and involvement in services, from social services to planning; from housing to schools. In general, between two-thirds and three-quarters of people want more say. Interestingly it was in the East Sussex study of social services that there was the least number who wanted it for *themselves* - just under half - although more than two-thirds had favoured a greater say for service users and local people more generally. Different groups seemed to have different demands and expectations. Old and middle-aged people were less likely to want more involvement. Those who particularly wanted more say tended to be members of ethnic minorities, families with children and young people.

So the indications from this evidence, and there is more both from research and participatory projects in a variety of fields including housing, social security, social services, medical care and so on, are that many people want to have more control over the services they and other people receive. However there is another issue here too, and it draws us back to those assumptions that people should not be troubled with all the burdens of involvement.

How to involve people

Whether people will get involved and want to get involved depends on what involvement *means*. We found in our large-scale study of planning and participation that efforts to involve people in local services, unintentionally or otherwise, tended to have race, gender, age and class biases. If we want to achieve a more broad-based involvement then it must be offered on people's own terms. We have got to stop mimicking the models of traditional policy development, which so often happens unconsciously, and search for more appropriate forms and processes. These must also be accompanied by the kinds of safeguards that will assure people it is actually *worth* getting involved in the first place and that their views will not just be taken away to be filed or re-interpreted. Only then are we likely to move beyond the small core of token or professional consumers or activists speaking for the rest of us, which tends to be the common situation now, and which can be used as an argument for restricting access even further.

Perhaps because of the poverty of much of the debate about participation, there is a tendency for such involvement to be seen as monolithic. However it is far from an all or nothing affair. Not only are there different degrees of participation, from consultation to an executive say, but there are different spheres for involvement in social services, including participation in one's own case, in the running and management of services and in their planning and development. There are also different settings for it - residential, fieldwork, domiciliary and day care - each of which would affect the nature and forms of involvement. Personal social services also pose particular issues for increased user participation and these need to be addressed. For example, contact with social services is often temporary or sporadic rather than continuous. How would consumer involvement be maintained? Would it be possible to avoid the involvement of users at one time conflicting with the wants and needs of users at another?

Questions like these often seem to have frightened commentators away from pursuing a democratic approach to consumer involvement. The explanation may lie, in part at least, in a larger issue: the very limited role of citizenship in our society. Because most of us are able to play so little part in local life and services, there seems to be a concern that the result will be to deluge people with enormous and probably unpleasant duties and responsibilities. In a society like ours where public participation is so difficult and restricted, that may be the case for the public-spirited or 'busybodying' minority who get involved. But extending user involvement should have the opposite effect.

We would not have to be involved in everything all the time. Our participation could have a beginning and an end. It might last only as long as we were using social services or trying to get day care for our under-fives. Flexibility should be the byword, allowing people to withdraw and get involved again according to other demands and developments in their lives. Participation could be tailored to meet our own individual preferences. We may only want a say in our own case, while the preparedness of others to take part in the planning and development of services would make sure that remained possible. At another time we might want to be more involved.

There is no reason why being involved should be dreary and unpleasant. Recently in a report they wrote about an attempt to involve people in deciding what services Family Service Unit should provide, a group of tenants spoke of the general sadness as well as great sense of achievement there was when the work was coming to an end [7]. Resources and support services would be needed to avoid unnecessary obstacles to people's participation, offering, for instance, child care, an attendance service, travelling expenses and accessible transport for people with disabilities. Most important, training for participation would be needed. Involvement is not the norm in our society. Most of us are ill-equipped to make the most of such opportunities. We need training to increase our confidence, gain new skills and develop old ones, find out how to acquire information and learn to work in groups.

Implications of consumer involvement
I would now like to look at some of the ramifications of listening to the voice of the consumer. First, if services are more closely based on what people want then we may expect them to change. Let us take one

example, the tendency of some social services to segregate and congregate people. This is to be seen in provision like adult training centres for people with mental handicaps, day centres for old people and workshops for people with disabilities. There is some evidence, for instance, that those using old people's lunch clubs and day centres like them, but that a larger proportion of old people prefer not to use them [8]. If as users we have a more active part in shaping the services on offer, it is to be expected that we may decide to change some of them.

There is a second implication for social services arising from this. There may also be changes in *who* uses them. At present that use tends to be relatively narrow. They are used by a larger percentage of people in certain groups, notably old people, but essentially their clientele is comparatively small. This can make for an important difference between them and other public services like education or health. Because use is statistically unusual and may also be associated with stigma and disrepute, social services users may be seen to be different from other people. Their interests and those of other members of the community may sometimes appear to conflict, and in some cases, of course, they do conflict. We should remember this because any process of listening to consumer views must make possible negotiation between them and other citizens as well as between different types of users themselves.

However, in my view, if more of us were involved in the shaping of social services, it is likely that we would seek to change them to meet the needs of more people. Then there would be a much greater overlap between us as service users, local people, carers, workers and others, reducing any artificial differences that traditional social services may have created between us as citizens and service users. The best known example of this perhaps is day care provision for under-fives. In most authorities this has been provided as a specific service for families seen as at 'high risk'. There is, however, a large demand from women for a more widely available, catchment-based service. Such an approach to social services, the probable corollary of steps towards their democratisation, could well make social service users of us all. There are, after all, enough services they could provide that any of us might need at some time, including bereavement counselling, advice on ageing, caring and neighbouring, assertion training, and much more besides. Social services users are not a separate marginal group. Who they are depends on *what* is provided and that in turn depends on *who* provides it.

In pursuing the goal of involvement, it would be mistaken to restrict our attention to consumers. Our commitment should extend to *all three* of the key groups involved - service users, workers and other local people. A preoccupation with only one of these constituencies, whichever it is, is likely to be divisive as well as less effective in the long run. There are two issues here. Not only does everyone have a right to a say in services, whether it is the services they use, work in or where they live, but it is only through such involvement that the negotiation of differences between them is likely to be possible. In my experience, exclusion and the powerlessness that goes with it are crucial causes of conflict and discrimination between disadvantaged people.

There is another implication for social services raised by increasing citizen-involvement. It is not just that democratisation could mean changed services for more people. Inherent in it also is a different distribution of *power*. Social services departments are organised on the basis of a hierarchy of power. They are also subject to the control of a political authority. While the balance between the hierarchy and politicians may have changed over the years, the balance between them and service users and other local people has not significantly altered, even in left-Labour authorities where there has been particular discussion of democratisation in the context of proposals for decentralisation. The latter have sometimes been the battleground for struggles between heads of different departments, managers and grassroots workers. Generally arguments for more accountable decentralised services have not extended to changes in the existing political and administrative structure, even if sometimes additional public forums have been created to sit alongside them.

Why should we expect the present power holders in social services to give any of that power away as they would be doing if the voice of service users were to be made more effective? If there is a reason, then it lies in the changing circumstances of social services departments as of other public services. As became very clear from the people we spoke to in our East Sussex study, social services mainly serve a *residual* role. I would argue that we can now expect social services departments to be further marginalised. Already some of their services have been taken over by the commercial sector. It does not seem mistaken to expect to see further pressures for other responsibilities to be off-loaded to charitable and other non-statutory services. The social services department may take on more of a coordinating and regulatory role, but it is itself likely to become a diminishing empire. If that happens, its directors and chairs will see *their* power reduced.

A new philosophy for social services
This surely is the time to begin to debate and develop a new philosophy for social services. If the threat is for power to be abrogated to the centre, does it not make sense to try devolving it to citizens and service users? This may actually offer the basis for challenging the rundown of social services. It is not a question of seeking the support of local people to 'fight the cuts' - one of the more facile arguments for the large-scale local government decentralisations of the early 1980s. Instead it is a matter of offering people a real sense of involvement so that they begin to experience a closer relation between their needs and services.

In our 1978 study of local authority planning and participation we encountered a strong and widespread distrust of the council coupled with dissatisfaction with its services. That legacy of paternalistic policy and provision remains. But it could be argued that constraints and cuts on collective provision have made it more and more difficult for those services to make their own sensitive response to individual choice.

If we want to challenge this vicious circle facing social and other services, let us begin by learning from the last big development in both social services and local authority services more generally - decentralisation. It was usually carried out on a large scale with grandiose claims and expectations. It was often imposed from the top down, engendering opposition from both the workforce and community. Social services do not need any more 'big bangs'. What are needed are small steps towards change. The commitment to test the hypothesis that we may better be able to ensure individual choice through collective provision by enhancing citizen say in it, is a big enough step in itself. We should take the kind of small-scale initiatives for which even now there are still opportunities. The emphasis must be on modest, well-worked out and monitored development projects, instead of the large-scale, ill-thought out and often retrospectively researched schemes that have typified decentralisation. We need to develop criteria which can offer us the basis for extending such schemes if and when it becomes possible. But, even in the short term, pilot projects like these need not be based on a residual role for services. On a small scale at local level, through increased citizen involvement, we can explore and try out more universalist services and provision.

It is also important to avoid a trend that can already be seen towards what we might call the professionalisation of initiatives for citizen involvement, where it is the same old officers, consultants and researchers who shape the agendas, influence the forms that are used and are the arbiters of the findings. Instead, the discussion about and development of such projects should itself be designed more carefully to draw in the experience, perspective and contribution of service users and other local people themselves. Just as we must avoid the problem posed by paternalist services, of one group deciding for another, be it men for women, or white for black people, so where the aim is to democratise services, priority must be given to supporting people's own account of their needs and wants rather than imposing others.

It is not that 'the voice of the consumer' has recently become louder or that there is suddenly greater demand for involvement. We found such a demand ten years ago. Ironically what seems to be happening is that as effective constraints on citizen participation in policies have increased, 'consumer views' have come to the forefront as an issue in the narrow social policy debate. What we need to guard against is their being reduced to an area of study or to mere information for the policy makers instead of serving as an element in the democratisation of services.

Advocates like myself of a democratic approach to consumer involvement in social services can expect to be criticised as idealistic and unrealistic. They will find themselves required to have ready answers to all the great questions of democracy long neglected in our society. For instance, is a more active model of citizenship what people actually want? If so, how is it to be achieved and how would it be reconciled with existing political institutions? The new consumerism presents a much more pragmatic and politic face. But if we wish to listen to the voice of the consumer, the same large questions of how to ensure public accountability and make people's participation possible face us *whatever* approach we advocate. Consumerism offers no short cuts and cannot itself duck the issue. It has to confront it too. Its exponents must find ways of overcoming the market's pull to inequality and centralisation, just as those of more democratic services must offer practical arguments for progressing their project.

References

1. Peter Beresford and Suzy Croft, *Whose Welfare: Private care or public services?*, Social Services and the Community Action Research Project, Lewis Cohen Urban Studies Centre, 1986.

2. 'Decentralisation in Southwark', Paper for the Policy Committee, London Borough of Southwark, 23 February 1987.

3. Peter Beresford and Suzy Croft, *A Say In The Future: Planning, participation and meeting social need*, Battersea Community Action, 1978.

4. See, for example, Peter Beresford and Suzy Croft, 'Intermediate Treatment, Special Education and the Personalisation of Urban Problems', in *The Practice of Special Education*, W. Swann (editor), Basil Blackwell/OUP, 1981; 'It's not much of a prospect', *Community Care*, 10 October 1981; 'It's a boy's life', in *Girls are Powerful*, S. Hemmings (editor), Sheba, 1982; 'Power, politics and the Youth Training Scheme', *Youth and Policy*, Vol. 2, No. 1, Summer 1983; 'Powerless in Toytown' and 'Plug in to the power supply', *Youth in Society*, December 1980 and January 1981.

5. Peter Beresford, Jane Tunstill and John Kemmis, *In Care in North Battersea*, University of Surrey, 1987.

6. See (1) *op.cit.*

7. We Can Speak for Ourselves, South Birmingham Family Service Unit, 1987.

8. See, for example, *Growing Old in Brighton: A Development Group exercise in Brighton 1977-79*, DHSS, Social Work Service

Development Group and Social Work Service Southern Region, East Sussex County Council Social Services Department, HMSO, 1980.

6. Collaboration with Consumers: Learning How to Listen

Adrianne Jones

Director of Social Services, City of Birmingham

Introduction

The arrival of consumerism as a new force in our social policy is something for which we should be grateful. Consumerism in personal social services is self-evidently a 'good thing'. It commands a broad political consensus and offers the possibility of a new vision for the weary and embattled personal social services. What is remarkable is not that consumerism's day has come now but rather that it has not come before. And we should pause to wonder why.

Consumerism was not a feature of the personal social services when we were planning for growth. It has come into its own during a period of retrenchment, both financially and politically. And it is the consensus which has encouraged consumerism to flourish that may, in time, prove to be a cause of its failure. Consumerism, rather like community care, is a strategy which appears to unite left, centre and right. But this apparent consensus obscures the enormous political and ideological differences from which consumerism emanates. If consumer-led strategies for the personal social services are to endure, then the ideological foundations must be explicit. We should avoid drawing too close an analogy with the market place because personal social services

53

development is not based on a model of consumer-driven market forces but on a complex combination of political mandate - what professionals deem appropriate according to their understanding of the problem, statutory requirements and so on.

But in practical terms, what does consumerism mean? Who are our consumers? Obviously they are those who receive our services - our clients - but the other group whose claims as consumers must be recognised are 'carers'. As we all know, most of the community care received by the majority of disabled people is provided by another member of their household - their informal carer.

A consumer-led strategy

A consumer-led strategy for personal social services also implies:

(a) that we know from our consumers what they want;

(b) that we know what their carers (paid and unpaid) consider that they need;

(c) that we are able to devise a pattern of service which represents a carefully negotiated balance between these two sets of views;

(d) that services are available when our consumers need them;

(e) that the service is delivered in an acceptable way;

(f) (most important) that our services provide a stepping stone rather than an obstacle to participation in the life of the community, as a full and valued citizen. Choice and consumer control are inseparable partners.

So consumerism becomes both a means to more effective and sensitive service delivery but it also stands as an end in itself.

Against this background, we must consider whether we are actually prepared for the scale of revolution in our existing practices that the achievement of a consumer-led approach to planning, development and delivery of services would actually entail. And critically, do we have evidence of the necessary political backing, public support and professional enthusiasm to renegotiate the balance of power and authority with our consumers?

I assume that we, as individuals who are managers and social policy makers, are enthusiastic about a new and more equal partnership with our consumers. But many of us preside over large organisations, whose systems for service delivery are often blatantly unsympathetic and indifferent to the human sensitiveness of our clients

- Why otherwise might a mentally handicapped person, not knowing that the driver is ill and the service was cancelled wait all day for the bus, which never arrives, to take him to the Adult Training Centre?

- Why are home helps instructed to separate the clients' ironing from the 'carers', and to refuse to clean upstairs because the 'client' cannot climb stairs?

- Why have we allowed our day services to shut at 4 pm on Friday afternoons when weekends are often the loneliest times?

- Why do we tolerate having elderly people in our residential care put to bed at 5 o'clock in the afternoon?

The Birmingham Community Care Special Action Project
But clearly the awakening of our professional and managerial consciousness to consumerism dates back to the early 1970s when we called it clients' rights. As a result of changes then, we now have client access to files, parents' attendance at Section 3 Resolution Hearings, clients' attendance at case conferences, and so on. But I suspect that all these developments have been more significant to professionals than they have been to clients. Hence our continued commitment is needed to see through the revolution that consumerism in its true form will herald. Because first and foremost the transformation involves the creation of a new service culture, underpinned by a determination to revalue explicitly the people who are our consumers, who invariably lead their lives at the margin of our society - their marginalisation often reinforced by the service we offer.

Through Birmingham City Council's initiative - the Community Care Special Action Project - we have devised a set of principles which provide a good framework from which to develop a consumer-led approach. These service principles are:

(i) People who have special needs because they are elderly, have a mental handicap, mental illness or a physical disability, should be valued as full citizens with both rights and responsibilities. They are entitled to be consulted and have an opportunity to influence the pattern of services on which they depend, to meet their individual and changing needs.

(ii) People with special needs should have access to services which promote the greatest degree of self-determination, on the basis of informed and realistic choice.

(iii) People with special needs have a right to support and participation in the community which does not exploit or disadvantage others.

(iv) People with special needs have a right of access to services which support their participation as valued members of the community. The services should be free of stigma associated with their use [1].

Practical strategies

Obviously, there are already developments in our current practice which will provide a basis for training through which these principles can be turned into a series of practical strategies for the development of a consumer-led service. These initiatives include:

(i) *Decentralisation* - reducing the distance between the point of service management and the point of use. Also, a move to closer working relationships between service providers and service receivers, together with a move to open up the range of generic services through decentralisation will be welcomed by our consumers. Most mentally handicapped people, as we know, do not want to spend every day with other people who are also mentally handicapped.

(ii) *The Disabled Persons Act 1986* - even though the timing for its full implementation is still uncertain, we should welcome this legislation as providing a further statutory anchor for increased access to information and service by consumers and carers.

(iii) *Complaints services* - these have had a mixed outcome and we need to explore with our consumers the reasons why. The more obvious causes we can speculate about - for example, that it is difficult to complain about a professional with whom you have continuing one-to-one contact, or that the complaints system may not be independent of the service it is intended to monitor.

(iv) *Partnership with the voluntary sector* - given their professed ambition for innovation, many voluntary organisations could provide a valuable lead in experimenting with structures which would give consumers opportunities to participate in and, indeed, *direct* policy making and planning. Because voluntary organisations tend to be small and potentially more flexible, we should seek from them a lead in this area. But at the same time we must not fall into the trap of believing that voluntary organisations necessarily represent 'consumer interests'. The growing professionalisation of the voluntary sector has made this increasingly less likely.

An important qualification to the capacity of voluntary organisations to act as 'consumer representatives' is that, in many cases, they may be major service providers, and therefore, in terms of representing the consumer interest, there may be a potential conflict of interest between professional and managerial determination and the exercise of consumer preference. Consumerism in the personal social services is essentially concerned with providing a framework which is more responsive and more guided by the views and attitudes of those who use our services. The minimum aim must be to draw our service provision more in line with expressed consumer need, rather than the other way round. Such a re-alignment will not produce a hopelessly impractical chaos of service responses. By and large, in our experience, consumers' horizons are rather broader than just social services. They do not think in neat departmental terms, nor do they think in terms of their needs existing only during the working day.

(v) Particular consideration must be given to hearing *the voice of consumers from ethnic minorities*. Here our state of knowledge is incomplete, but, again, the principles for beginning to develop a consumer-led approach remain the same. Through the Special Action Project, we hope to be collaborating with the King's Fund Informal Caring Support Unit in the development of a small-scale action project, which will investigate the needs of Asian carers. Non-English speaking carers have been noticeably absent from our Special Action Project's meetings for carers, despite our distribution of translated posters and advertising of the availability of translators at each meeting.

Future developments

So how can we develop this fairly familiar agenda? And how else can we learn how to listen? In answer to that, we must begin by asking ourselves as senior managers some hard questions. When did we last sleep in one of our homes for elderly people? When did we last have a conversation or a meal with a group of people who are mentally handicapped? When did we last sit in the reception area of one of our local offices? Perhaps this is where we can start.

Because the voice of the consumer must be heard at every level within our organisations, it must not be hushed by the protocol of line management. We should listen to what people say, and ask ourselves: 'Would this be good enough for me? Would I choose to live here? Would I enjoy spending my day here?' While this highly subjective judgement is not a perfect planning tool, it will certainly do in the short term.

And of course, learning to listen to our consumers will also mean that we will hear things which are profoundly discomforting, that confront us with our impotence, incompetence, with our insensitivity. In Birmingham we have launched a series of open meetings with carers. Soon we will launch similar services for consumers, and over the next three years we will, on three or four occasions each year, hold open meetings for carers in each of the five districts into which the city is divided. The purpose of these meetings is to hear from carers about their good or bad experiences in relation to:

(i)   getting a break;

(ii) getting help at home.

Assistance with each meeting is recruited from a wide range of agencies, with small groups led by senior managers, in order to spread the benefit and impact of this important exercise in the services feedback. One District General Manager, who had led a group of carers at one of our most recent consultations, described the experience as 'deeply moving' as he said, 'I heard about our services from these carers in terms that never survive transmission up the hierarchy'.

And what have we learnt so far from what we have heard?

(i) We have learnt about the considerable concern among carers about the quality of what we provide. For some, what is seen by them as the poor quality of some of our services means that they are not acceptable. Disturbingly, the services may collude with this. One lady, caring for an elderly neighbour, told us how she had sought help from her local social services office. The only alternative on offer - residential care - was ruled out by the social worker, who said to her, 'You've destroyed her for a home - you've looked after her too well'.

(ii) We have heard from parents who have young physically disabled relatives, who would keep them at home rather than expose them to what they see as the unstimulating monotony of the day centre, offering only companionship with other disabled and much older people.

(iii) We have heard also how often our services are unavailable at the time when they are most needed. For example, when a frail or elderly person falls at night, it is the police who are called or, alternatively, the elderly person may be left on the floor, covered and cared for as well as possible until the home help arrives in the morning and the services open up once more.

(iv) And finally we have heard how little people ask for. Most people wish to continue to care but would like to have a break - for a few hours - not for their relative to be whisked off permanently to a Part III home.

So we begin to listen. How do we set about developing systems to ensure that a continuing flow of consumer response permeates the planning, management and delivery of our services at every level?

(i) *In planning* we want to look to the development of local consumer consortia - groups of users and interested lay people who will receive all information that is produced by local planning groups, and then will have an opportunity to comment and reflect on the nature of the proposals. This approach will overcome the problems of tokenism raised by the cooption of one or two service users onto central planning groups. The consumer consortia must, however, also recognise and reflect the differences of attitude often found between carers and service users. We must also ensure that the consumer consortia are properly serviced and administered.

(ii) *Build on decentralisation.* There is always, at least initially, the strong likelihood that true consumer voices will be lost in a forum which is dominated by people who are competent, as a result of experience and practice, in handling the procedure of meetings. Certainly, as a transitional strategy, informal groups of consumers should be invited together to comment on local service issues across a broad range.

(iii) *Building political support* - clients are also voters. But a positive action approach is also needed in the representation of consumer views. Just as white representatives may be unacceptable to some black communities, so non-handicapped people may not be adequate representatives of those who are handicapped. Advocacy schemes should be developed, to ensure that the voices of mentally handicapped people in particular are heard.

(iv) *Working in partnership with the trade unions.* This is critical from the outset. Because undertaking a consumer-led service strategy does imply substantial changes in existing working practices - the nature of the job done, the hours at which it is done and the skills required - greater consumer accountability must also be balanced by proper respect for rights of staff. For instance, at our carers' consultations, we make it an absolute rule that no member of staff is to be criticised by name, but any complaint, should it arise, should be channelled with assistance through the proper complaints procedure.

(v) *Training.* The implementation of a new service culture through training at every level. The focus of training approaches must be by revaluing disabled people and by supporting them to live ordinary lives in socially valued settings.

In many ways initiating this revolution will be a thankless task. We cannot expect our consumers to be grateful. More likely we will serve to mobilise the frustration of many years of anger.

Let us remember for a moment Alice in Wonderland: 'But I don't want to go among mad people,' Alice remarked. 'Oh you can't help that,' said the cat, 'We're all mad here. I'm mad. You're mad.' 'How do you know?' 'You must be,' said the cat, 'or you wouldn't have come here.'

So the process will not be tidy, it will not be orderly, but if we succeed in surrendering some of our professional monopoly for determining the outcome of our consumers' lives, we will have helped create some space for them to come alongside us in the mainstream of society.

Reference
1. *Community Care Special Action Project - Project Journal*, City of Birmingham Social Services Department, May 1987.